DAVY CROCKETT

DAVY CROCKETT

An American Hero

Tom Townsend

EAKIN PRESS
Austin, Texas

FIRST EDITION

Copyright © 1987
By Tom Townsend

Published in the United States of America
By Eakin Press, P.O. Box 23069, Austin, Texas 78735

ISBN 0-89015-643-3

Library of Congress Cataloging-in-Publication Data

Townsend, Tom.
    Davy Crockett : an American hero.

    Bibliography: p.
    Includes index.
    Summary: Follows the life of the renowned pioneer, with an emphasis on his experiences on the American frontier in the early nineteenth century.
    1. Crockett, Davy, 1786–1836—Juvenile literature. 2. Pioneers—Tennessee—Biography—Juvenile literature. 3. Legislators—United States—Biography—Juvenile literature. 4. United States. Congress. House—Biography—Juvenile literature. 5. Crockett, Davy, 1786–1836. 6. Pioneers. 7. Frontier and pioneer life. I. Title.
F436.C95T68   1987   976.8'04'0924 [B] [92]   87-16545
ISBN 0-89015-643-3

For the late Howard Simpson . . .
hunter, fisherman, dreamer,
and a kindred spirit
of Davy Crockett.

Preface

Davy Crockett was a frontiersman, a politician, and a folk hero of great popularity. But most people remember him for his heroism and valiant death at the Battle of the Alamo.

Inside the Alamo chapel today are a few things which remain of Davy Crockett: a lock of his hair, a tin box, and a beard brush. There is even a log from his cabin in Tennessee. The rifle he called Old Betsy is there, although it is much changed since the day Davy last fired it. There is even a reproduction of his coonskin cap.

Most everything else we know, or think we know, about Davy Crockett is a collection of educated guesses. We are not absolutely sure that his body was burned in a funeral pyre along with those of the other Alamo defenders. There are at least five different reported locations where those ashes were supposed to have been buried later.

The experts will argue forever about the details of the exact way he died. They will argue his reasons for coming to Texas and for remaining at the Alamo. They will even doubt that he actually wore a coonskin cap (it may have been made from the skin of a fox instead).

To have told only the known facts about David Crockett would have made a very short and very dull book. When it had been read, the reader would know very little about the real man.

To have collected all of the theories, guesses, legends, and wild stories about Davy Crockett would have filled the shelves of a library. And after all of those books were read, the readers would still have to form their own opinions about what kind of person Davy Crockett really was, what things he really did, what hat he really wore, and how he really died.

This book was intended to do neither of the above. Instead, it was intended to paint a picture of the life of Davy Crockett as this author sees it after months of research. I have used the known facts whenever they exist. Wherever possible, I have used his own words. But when those words were lost to history, I recreated them as I believe he would have spoken them. In some cases I even invented a name for a character or two whom Davy wrote about in his autobiography but did not name.

I also used some of the legends and wild stories whenever I believed they could have really happened. This is my way of making Davy Crockett as real as possible.

1

Davy Crockett figures that, at best, he has about three hours to live. With one dirty hand, he pushes the coonskin cap farther back on his head and looks up at the night sky. A million stars seem to hang there, just beyond his reach. He has watched them all during the long night, and now Sirius, the brightest of them all, has worked its way close to the western horizon. There cannot be more than two hours left before dawn. After that, he reckons he'll be dead in no time.

An icy north wind whistles through the walls of the old mission outside San Antonio de Bexar and chills him beneath his ragged buckskin clothing. From his crouched position on the south wall, Davy can see the campfires of the Mexican army. Like stars fallen to the ground, they are spread out nearly as far as the eye can see. For days their reinforcements have been arriving from across the Rio Grande. Now, about 5,000 men of the best-trained and best-equipped army in North America face 180 ragtag Texans entrenched behind these battered walls of the Alamo.

For twelve days the little garrison has held out

against the constant pounding of the Mexican artillery. Only since nightfall have the guns been silent.

Crockett reasons that, for him at least, there could be many worse places to die than here, in battle for a cause in which he so strongly believes. He is in gallant company, for behind these ancient walls are some of the greatest fighters of the day.

There are fifteen men from Davy's home state of Tennessee. Many of them fought in the Creek Indian War with him over twenty years ago.

Jim Bowie, perhaps the most famous knife fighter in all of the world, is here. And Col. William Barret Travis, young, bold, and fanatically loyal, is the Alamo's commander. During his twenty-six years of life, he has been an English teacher, a lawyer, and now a colonel in the revolutionary army of Texas. Glory and honor seem foremost in his mind, and he has sworn a bloody oath that there will be no retreat and no surrender. Davy suspects he is a man with many secrets.

There is Capt. Almeron Dickinson, who arrived two weeks ago with thirty-two men from Gonzales. With him has come his young wife, Susanna, and their daughter Angelina. Like Davy, they had come to Texas from Tennessee with dreams of free land and wide open spaces. Dickinson also once served with Davy under Gen. Andrew Jackson during the Creek Indian War.

A few scattered clouds race before the north wind, and for a moment they hide the crescent moon. Davy closes his eyes. Perhaps there is still time left to think, to try and sort out some of his forty-nine years of life.

He rubs his hand lovingly across the cold steel of the Kentucky long rifle cradled in the crook of his left arm. The rifle has always been such an important part of his life.

Images of the green hills of Tennessee float into his mind's eye. He sees the little log cabin, deep in the wilderness on Big Limestone River, where he was born on

August 17, 1786. The scene fades and dissolves to the tavern that his father built on the road between Knoxville and Abingdon. Yes, perhaps it was there that it really began, at least the important parts. It was there that David Crockett met Jacob Siler.

* * *

The smoke from a dozen clay pipes hung in a heavy gray haze about the common room of John Crockett's tavern. Hickory wood blazed and popped in the big fireplace, which took up most of one wall. The odors of tobacco and wood smoke mingled with those of whiskey, dark ale, and fresh roasted venison. Candlelight flickered against the log walls and sent dancing shadows among the rough-hewn beams of the low ceiling.

The customers were mostly wagoners. With wagons they owned themselves, these men hauled sugar, flour, barrels of molasses, and other basic items needed by the settlers along the western frontier of Tennessee. They would return to the East in wagons heavily loaded with corn, rye, and other farm produce to feed the growing cities. They were a rough and rowdy lot, but there was a friendly fellowship among them. As with sailors and soldiers, there was a kinship born out of the adventure and danger that they all faced. The roads they traveled were barely trails through the wilderness. There were no bridges across the swift rivers, which could carry away their wagons and teams. Blizzards froze them in winter and sudden storms in spring washed out the roads or covered them with landslides. And, of course, there was always the danger of Indians.

Twelve-year-old David Crockett staggered under a double armload of firewood as he weaved his way among the customers.

"The lad's quirky," he heard his father telling someone in the corner. "Most probable, he won't never amount ta a hill-o-beans."

3

David tried to ignore the comment. No matter how hard and long he worked, nothing he did ever seemed to please his father. In fact, there seemed to be nothing to look forward to in life except more hard, endless work. The travelers' horses had to be stabled and fed. Water had to be hauled for the kitchen. More firewood had to be chopped and split and then stacked on the hearth.

Another voice, one with a strange accent, which David had never heard before, was answering his father. "He is *gut* boy. He listens to his elders und learns from dem. Much like da little ones I remember from da old country."

"Reckon that's about the only good thing I ever heard said 'bout me," David thought as he dropped the firewood onto the stone hearth. He sneaked a glance at the corner table. Beside David's father sat a solemn-faced man with sandy hair and a bushy mustache. There was a pewter mug of ale in one big fist. His eyes were a brilliant blue and seemed to pierce into his very soul. David turned away quickly and started for the door.

"Get yourself over here, boy," his father's gruff voice halted him.

"Aw, heck," David whispered to himself as he turned around and started toward the table in the corner. "I reckon I'm in fur it now."

There was a long moment of awkward silence as David stood in front of the two men. "This here's Mr. Siler, Mr. Jacob Siler. He's drivin' a few head uh beef north up Pennsylvania way."

As David nodded his head, his eyes fell on a rifle that lay on the table in front of Jacob Siler. It was beautiful, David thought. The barrel looked as big as a cannon and the stock was a golden blond wood, polished and oiled until it looked more like a piece of jewelry than a weapon. There were pictures of birds and deer and mountains, and all matter of designs inlaid with bright silver on the barrel and lock. David could have admired the weapon

4

for hours, but his father's next words shocked him back to the harsh reality of frontier life.

"You're bound out to Mr. Siler now. You work hard, do what he tells ya, and he'll pay five dollars when ya get up ta Pennsylvania. Now, get yer things together, you'll be leavin' come first light."

David's mouth dropped open but he could say nothing. He did not even know where Pennsylvania was, except it was somewhere far to the north, and he was sure it would take weeks or months to get there driving cattle.

"Yes, sir," David finally managed to answer as he turned to leave and cast one more look at Jacob Siler's beautiful rifle.

2

A shadow moves among the cottonwood trees, about one hundred yards away. Davy cocks the hammer of his long rifle and steadies the barrel across the top of the wall. Mexican scouts are trying to get a closer look at the Texans' defenses. Davy waits, silent and still as stone. Patience, he knows from long experience, is usually the answer in a situation like this; wait and make the enemy move first.

The moon slips from behind a cloud. Its pale light bathes the land with a cold, eerie glow. The shadow moves again. A man, running in a low crouch, darts from the trees, moving ever closer to the walls. Davy tightens his finger on the trigger. The Texans have no friends beyond the walls tonight.

The shadow is in the open now, still running in a stooped position. Davy leads his target and aims a little high. There is a tendency to shoot low in moonlight. Old words, lessons learned long ago in the rolling hills of Pennsylvania, echo in his mind: "Shoot mit da whole body. Become one mit da rifle; your eyes are da barrel. Shoot vere you look!"

The hammer falls. A long tongue of orange flame leaps from the barrel and "Old Betsy" jumps in his hands. White smoke, bright and unreal in the moonlight, sweeps over him. One hundred and fifty yards away, the running shadow tumbles forward. A distant scream pierces the night as the shadow rolls a few yards and then lies still in an untidy heap with arms and legs extended in unnatural directions.

Davy lowers his rifle. The image of Jacob Siler's stern face floats before him, silently nodding his approval. It had been with Mr. Siler's beautiful German rifle that Davy Crockett once learned the fine art of shooting.

* * *

Jacob Siler and young David Crockett had left John Crockett's tavern an hour before the autumn sun had peeked over the hazy ridges of the Great Smoky Mountains. Siler's Conestoga wagon followed the small herd of cattle as they slowly pushed northward day after day.

Siler, David learned, was a man of few words. David had long ago learned that where grownups were concerned, it was usually best to speak only when spoken to. As the days passed, David said little and worked hard, herding the cattle and attending to all the chores that Siler assigned to him. Slowly, as they made their way ever northward, he earned the old German's respect.

David also learned that Siler was the finest marksman he had ever known. The old German could bring down a deer running through the forest or a wild turkey in flight. His aim was always true, and the beautiful rifle never left his hands. During the day, it was carried across his lap as he drove the wagon. At night he slept with it cradled in his arms.

They continued north, leaving the hazy outline of the Smoky Mountains behind and climbing into the Blue Ridge range. Day by day, David became more fascinated by Siler's marksmanship.

7

One night they camped high in the Blue Ridge Mountains. Only a few bones remained of the fat rabbit they had eaten for supper, and the campfire burned low. Jacob sat with his back against a tall pine tree, contentedly cleaning his rifle. He rubbed oil into the barrel and firing lock, then carefully wiped away any excess. After that, he would polish the wooden parts with a fine mixture of oil and soot.

"In da wilderness, your gun is your life," he told the boy. "You take care of it just like you take care of yourself."

"You reckon you could learn me ta shoot your rifle?" David asked suddenly.

Jacob stopped his polishing and stared at the boy for a long moment. Then he huffed and said only, "Ve vill see."

As the weeks passed and the journey continued, the forests of the Blue Ridge gave way to the rolling hills of Pennsylvania. They arrived at last, at the home of Jacob's son-in-law. It was here that old Jacob Siler had decided to make his home. He gave David six dollars and told him he was quite pleased with his work.

There was a tiny twinkle in the man's eyes when he said, "I vant you should stay a while longer und work mit me here. Dere is much to get done before da vinter snows come."

David's thoughts had been of home, and he wanted very much to get back to the Tennessee hills.

Jacob rubbed a hand over his rifle. "I think dere vould be some time to teach you to shoot like a German," he added with a little smile. The deal was done. David would stay "a while longer," and he would learn the finer points of using a rifle.

Shooting was not new to young David Crockett. Since he had been eight years old, his father had sent him into the forest to shoot meat for supper. Carrying an old smooth-bore musket, he was given only one ball and one charge of powder. With this single shot, he was expected to bring home meat for the family table. If he missed the rabbit, wild turkey, or raccoon at which he fired, he would be sent to bed without supper.

Today those lessons seem harsh and cruel. But on the Tennessee frontier in the 1780s, a man's skill with his rifle was most important. It supplied his food and protected him from Indians. With it, he also had to protect his own farm animals from roving wolves and foxes. There was no excuse for being a poor shot.

The lessons that David learned from Jacob Siler went far beyond the basic principles of marksmanship. He learned first how to take care of his rifle. He learned where to apply the oil, and that too much oil was often just as bad as not enough.

"Think of your rifle as a part of you. Don't abuse it no more than you vould a pet dog dat you love," Jacob told him many times.

It was several long days before David was allowed to actually shoot the rifle. Over and over again, Jacob made him practice aiming. He talked of something called "leading the target" and something else the Germans called "easy swing."

"Dere must be time for your brain to tell your finger to pull da trigger, time for da hammer to fall and da powder to explode. So, if da bird is moving, you must shoot in front of him. Und you must follow through, keep the rifle moving even after you have pulled da trigger."

Germans are rarely gentle teachers. But lessons learned from them are often remembered for a lifetime. "No, no! Dat is all wrong!" Jacob screamed when the boy missed his target. "Look mit da barrel; see da target mit da barrel!"

Even when David hit his target, Jacob might not be satisfied. He caught every little mistake. Always. "You are pushing your left hip too far forward. You shoot like a little girl!"

9

David listened and learned, for there was nothing in the world he wanted more than to be a fine shot. In the days which followed, he was allowed to take the rifle with him for daily hunting. He practiced everything Jacob had taught him, always improving his skill and style. Before the winter snows came, he decided that if he could someday "be his own man and carry his own rifle," then he would be satisfied with his life.

Slowly, young David's thoughts again turned homeward. The little tavern on the Abingdon Road seemed very far away. It had been many months since he had seen his mother, father, sisters, and brothers. He missed them very much.

Jacob plainly did not want him to leave. He would always say, "Stay a little longer. Work with me here." David might well have done that, for he respected the old German and loved using his fine rifle. Fate, however, had other plans for David Crockett.

A light snow had fallen one Sunday morning as he was walking back along the road from an early hunt. Two squirrels were slung over his shoulder, and the rifle was cradled in his arm. Three Conestoga wagons, drawn by teams of oxen, rounded the corner in front of him.

The lead wagon rattled to a stop and its driver called down: "Mornin' friend. How far be it to the next place we might find lodging for the night?"

"Tavern be a fair piece on down the road, 'bout seven mile I reckon," David told him.

The driver squinted one eye and took a long look at the boy. "What be yer name, lad?"

"David Crockett, sir."

"Yer pa be the John Crockett who keeps a tavern down Abingdon way?"

At first David was too surprised to answer. Then he remembered that the wagoner, Amos Dunn, and his sons had often stopped at Crockett's tavern.

"Where ya headed?" David asked, seeing a chance to go home.

"Clear down ta Knoxville," Mr. Dunn said. "We'll be passin' your pa's tavern on the way."

David made his decision. He wanted to go home, and here was his chance. "Could ya use another hand on the trip?" he asked.

Mr. Dunn assured him that he was welcome to come with them and said that they would be leaving the tavern at dawn the next day.

"I'll be there," David assured them and headed back to the house to gather up his things. At once he began to feel guilty about leaving Jacob, who had been so kind to him. But David had worked hard and done everything he had been asked to do. In fact, he had stayed much longer than he had originally agreed to. Yet somehow he doubted that he would be able to tell Jacob to his face that he was leaving.

As it turned out, he never had to. Since it was a Sunday afternoon when he got back to the house, the Silers were away visiting friends. When evening came, he rolled up his few belongings and hid them under his pillow. Then he put his six silver dollars in his pocket and went to bed with all his clothes on.

Everyone was sleeping soundly when he slipped from the house and closed the door quietly behind him. Eight inches of fresh snow lay on the ground. Blizzard winds drove blinding snowflakes all around him as he tucked his bedroll under his arm and turned up the collar of his coat. The night was pitch black. He had seven long miles to go before dawn, but that did not matter. David was going home.

3

Davy hears boots crunch on the broken ground behind him as smoke from Old Betsy drifts on the north wind toward the cottonwood trees along the river. He turns to see Colonel Travis, the Alamo's young commander, move beside him.

"Crockett, what was it?"

David finishes ramming ball and powder down Old Betsy's muzzle and primes the pan. "Jes' a Mexican scoutin' round. I figure there's maybe one more with him." He brings the hammer back to half-cock and pushes the long rifle's barrel back over the wall. "Reckon he'll git careless pretty soon too."

Travis raises his head carefully above the low, earthen wall that stretches between the southwest corner of the chapel and the low barracks of the west wall. He is a tall man with dark hair and piercing eyes, but the most outstanding thing about him is the fact that he is neat and well dressed. Days before the siege began, he ordered himself a complete new uniform. Davy can only wonder how his blue swallow-tail coat, white pantaloons, and brown boots have somehow remained spotless.

"This has to be the day they attack with everything," Travis comments as he looks out at the Mexican campfires. "It's the only possible reason Santa Anna would stop shelling us. He wants us all asleep when the attack comes."

"I'm feared you're probably right, Travis. Seein' as how they been shootin' at us with everything from cannons to muskets fur twelve days and nights now. They ain't hit nobody yet, so they gotta try somethin' before they run plum out of powder and shot."

"I just left Bowie," Travis says. "I think he'd like to see you."

"I been meanin' to do that." From the wall beside him, Davy picks up a pair of pistols and places them in his belt. He rises, carefully keeping his head low, and takes his rifle. Every bone in his body aches. He has not shaved in almost two weeks, and black powder stains his face and his buckskin clothing.

"Yes sirree," Davy mutters. "If ol' Mr. Kitchen could see me now, he'd figure he was right about me never amountin' ta nothin'."

"Kitchen?" Travis frowns, irritated that Crockett could think about anything except the 5,000 Mexican soldiers camped just beyond the walls.

"That was back when I was a shirt-tail kid of thirteen. My pa took it into his head that I ought ta get some book learnin'. Mr. Kitchen was my schoolteacher. We never got along too well."

With his rifle in hand, Davy starts across the yard toward the chapel. He passes a few men huddled around one of the tiny fires. As he nears the battered doors of the Alamo's chapel, it is as if he is walking toward the door of that little, one-room schoolhouse a couple of miles from Crockett's tavern, far away in Tennessee, in another time, another world.

* * *

There was something about Mr. Kitchen that re-

13

minded young David Crockett of one of the long-legged birds that waded in the shallows of the Nolochucky River. He was a tall, lanky man with a large nose that resembled a beak. Tiny, round-rimmed spectacles were perched there, and David had to wonder what kept them from falling off. He wore a frock coat, which was a bit too large for him, and breeches, which were a bit too small. One hand always held a hickory stick.

David made this observation carefully one fall afternoon as he peeked over the top of his *First Reader* while the older students were struggling with an exercise in spelling.

David had attended school for three days. Except for a few letters of the alphabet, about the only thing he had learned so far was the purpose of Mr. Kitchen's hickory stick. It had rapped painfully on his knuckles when he had forgotten what letter of the alphabet followed "E." It had stung his behind when he had been caught talking to his brother at a time he was supposed to be listening.

All in all, young David was finding that going to school was a lot harder than driving cattle, hunting wild game, or just about anything else he had ever done. And there were other problems besides Mr. Kitchen and his hickory stick.

Every school, it seems, has a bully. This school had Angus McGruffy. He was two years older than David, stood six inches taller, and weighed about fifty pounds more. He could eat as much as five boys or two men could. Angus worked very hard at being the school bully. He naturally picked a fight with every new boy. After he had left them with a black eye, a bloody nose, and maybe a couple of loose teeth thrown into the bargain, then they usually got along pretty well. Of course, Angus always took his choice of whatever they brought for lunch.

Angus also believed that no first-rate bully should have to do his own homework. So he made sure that someone did his papers and had them ready for him before school every morning. Even with all this planning, he still had to beat up on somebody every week or so, just to make sure they remembered he was the boss.

When Angus first saw thirteen-year-old David Crockett, he was not impressed. Angus had already fought three of his older brothers and they all seemed to be staying in line quite well. This new addition to the Crockett clan was the smallest of the lot—and also the most quiet. In fact, David was so quiet that Angus forgot he was there for three days.

"So you be little baby Crockett?" Angus sneered, using his toughest voice as he blocked the schoolhouse doorway after lunch. "Well, you sho'nuf be the runt o' the litter."

To David, Angus looked like a mountain—with ears. He tried to slip past him, but Angus grabbed his hair and pulled until it hurt.

"Why, I already had ta whup up on all yo brothers," Angus growled in his ear, "I reckon it's come time for me ta give ya a lickin' too, just so's ya know who be the toughest kid around here." With that, he released David's hair and kicked him in the seat of his pants.

Propelled by Angus's foot, David stumbled forward and tripped. Mr. Kitchen turned just in time to see him fall onto the schoolhouse floor. The schoolmaster's eyes moved from David to Angus, who shrugged innocently, and then back to David as he picked himself up.

"Master Crockett," Mr. Kitchen sighed, "I insist that you learn to enter this classroom on your feet."

"Yessir," David gulped and took his seat. For a long time, he sat with his fists clenched at his side and was so mad that his ears turned bright red.

"Ya can't fight 'em, David," his brother William whispered in his ear as soon as Mr. Kitchen turned around to the blackboard. "Jes' let 'em hit ya a couple a times an he'll leave ya alone then."

"He may whup me, but I sure ain't gonna make it no easier fur 'em," David whispered back through gritted teeth.

"Heck, little brother, he's done whupped up on every boy along the Abingdon Road. Why, he'll grind your face so far inta the dirt, come spring, we'll have ta plant ya fur corn."

David stuck out his chin. "Reckon I'll give 'em salt 'n vinegar afore he does."

As the afternoon passed, David made his plans. Any fight he would have with Angus McGruffy would have to be someplace away from the school. Win or lose, if Mr. Kitchen found out about it, there would be another beating. David had no intention of being beaten up by Angus and then getting the hickory stick too.

His chance came late that afternoon while Mr. Kitchen was busy with some of the other students. Moving as quietly as an Indian, Davy carefully picked up his books. He waited until Mr. Kitchen's back was turned and silently tiptoed out the door. Angus watched him go and whispered as he passed: "You can run, Crockett, but ya can't hide from me. An' when I find you, I'm gonna skin you alive."

David grinned at him and stuck out his tongue just as he backed out the door.

The school bell was still ringing when Angus raged out into the schoolyard looking for David. "I'll find that little rat and when I do, I'm gonna rip off his head and kick it clear ta Cumberland Gap."

"That little runt's probably still a runnin', Angus," another boy said as everyone watched the bully storming around the schoolyard, looking behind every tree and under every bush for the vanished young Crockett.

"Well, I reckon he best never show his face 'round here again or I'll give 'em what fur," Angus announced as he tucked his thumbs behind his suspenders. This had been the easiest victory he had ever had.

16

It occurred to him that he had reached a new height of success. He must be so terrible that boys like Crockett would run from his sight. It was all very satisfying, except for one thing: If David did not return to school, Angus would never get to eat his lunch. But, he reasoned, the Crocketts were poor and they never brought anything good for lunch anyway. Somewhat comforted by that thought, Angus and his company of cowering friends started off down the trail for home. They had gone just far enough that the schoolhouse was out of sight when they rounded a bend in the trail. There, standing in the middle of the road and calmly waiting for them, was David Crockett.

Angus stammered a little as he said, "I . . . I figured you'd still be a runnin'. Ya get lost or somethin?"

David started toward the bully.

"I think he's gonna fight ya, Angus," someone said in a surprised voice.

Angus did not have a chance to give the matter much thought. David flew into him like a mad rooster. His first blow landed on the end of Angus's nose and sent little stars of pain dancing before his eyes. As Angus's hands moved to protect his face, David kicked him in the shins and then stomped on his toes. When Angus bent over from the pain, David grabbed a handful of his hair and pulled for all he was worth until the bully fell forward. Like a small whirlwind, David jumped on top of Angus and kept on hitting and kicking as they rolled across the dusty path.

For a while it looked as if David might get the better of the big bully, but Angus's size and weight were a tremendous advantage. With one huge effort, he rolled on top of David and sat straddled across him. "Now I'm gonna teach ya who's the boss 'round here," he panted as he wiped blood from his nose and hit David in the face with his bloody fist.

17

"David flew into him like a mad rooster."

18

The blows rained down on David. Angus was in a fit of rage. He would teach this little runt a lesson he would remember for the rest of his life. David's head bounced against the hard ground. He saw Angus through a red haze of blood and rage, sitting above him and grinning as he struck again and again.

David's hands grabbed out desperately for any weapon in reach. His fingers clawed at the dirt until they gripped a large rock. With failing strength, he swung with the rock gripped tightly in his fist.

There was a hollow thud as the rock connected with Angus's forehead. The painful rain of fists stopped suddenly. Angus's eyes rolled back in his head, and his huge body began to sway from side to side.

David pushed him with all his might, and the bully toppled onto the ground. As he scrambled to his feet, David saw Angus crawling away in the dust. Running at him from behind, David planted his foot on the seat of his pants. The kick knocked Angus flat on his face, and before he could even roll over David was firmly planted on his back.

"Say uncle!" David panted as he ground the bully's face into the dirt. "Say uncle or I'll grind you into cornmeal!" Angus blubbered something and coughed. With both hands gripping his hair, David banged Angus's head against the ground again.

"Say uncle!" he repeated.

"Uncle, uncle!" the bully gasped. David stepped off of him.

"Don't you never mess with no Crocketts again, you hear?" David growled in his face and then turned away, leaving Angus lying in the path.

David got home that evening feeling about ten feet tall. He had whipped Angus McGruffy, the school bully. That, he suddenly realized, made David Crockett the new school bully. He whistled as he pitched hay for the horses and fed the pigs. He had carried in a couple of extra armloads of firewood before he began to wonder if Mr. Kitchen would find out about the fight. Angus had two black eyes, scratches all over his face, and a cut on his forehead where the rock had hit him. David did not look all that good himself, so the fight was not likely to remain a secret for long. Worst of all, if Angus was to tell Mr. Kitchen that David had hit him with a rock, then he would be in for a whipping for sure.

The more David thought about it, the more he began to worry. By sunrise the next morning, he had decided that it would not be wise for him to go back to school. Of course, it would also be an equally bad idea to tell his father that he was not going back to school.

David left for school that morning with his brothers just as if everything was normal. He walked with them about half of the way to the schoolhouse and then disappeared into the woods. There he remained all day until his brothers returned back down the road in the afternoon. This went on for three days before Mr. Kitchen began to wonder what had become of the young Crockett.

"We told 'em you was powerful sick," William said when they met that afternoon. "But he ain't gonna believe that fur ever. You better get on back ta school an take yer lickin' afore Pa finds out and wales ya a bunch worse."

Still, David could not bring himself to face the consequences of returning to school. For almost another week, he lay out in the woods every day. He was not enjoying his forced vacation one bit. There was nothing for him to do all day except worry about what was going to happen when, sooner or later, he got caught. The following Monday, Mr. Kitchen sent home a note with David's brother, asking Mr. Crockett how David was feeling. Once again, David was in trouble.

"Why the devil ain't you been goin' ta school, boy?" John Crockett yelled from behind the flagon of whiskey he was drinking.

"Scared to, Pa. Ol' Mr. Kitchen gonna whup me with his hickory stick an' cook me up to a cracklin', 'cause I busted Angus McGruffy's head with a rock."

John Crockett slammed down his drink and sent drops of corn whiskey across the table. His breath was heavy with the odor of liquor as he leaned close to his son. "Scared? Scared of a lickin'? Boy, you ain't never dreamed of no lickin' like I'm fixin' ta give ya if ya don't get your scrawny little tail down ta that schoolhouse."

"Aw, but Pa, I . . ." David started.

"Get, boy!"

David left the cabin but hesitated just outside the front door. He hesitated a bit too long. When his father came through the door, he was already good and mad. And there was the biggest hickory stick in his hand that David had ever seen.

David looked at the stick and then at his father, who had been drinking most of the night. There seemed to be nothing to do but run.

His father charged after him, swinging the hickory stick as he ran. David scampered off down the trail in the opposite direction of the dreaded schoolhouse, with his father in hot pursuit. The chase ran on for a mile or so, and at times David believed that his father might overtake him. But stark terror is a fine thing for getting that extra bit of speed just when it is needed. In David's case, the need came at the bottom of a long hill. By keeping up his speed all the way to the top, he had managed to put a little extra distance between him and his father.

Once over the top, he turned quickly to the side and dove beneath a large bush. Burrowing himself far inside the tangled leaves and branches, he waited. The sounds of heavy breathing grew louder as the old man topped the hill. His father's footsteps hurried past as a blue streak of curses and threats described in great detail what he would do to David when he caught him.

21

It was just about then that young David Crockett decided that it was going to be a long time before he could go home again.

But what was he to do now? Sadly, he picked himself up and started down the trail, away from the schoolhouse and away from home.

Jim Bowie may already be dead, Davy thinks as he steps into the tiny baptistery of the Alamo's chapel. A thin, silent figure, smelling of blood and sickness, lies beneath a blanket on a cot against the wall. One arm is across his chest, and the feeble light of a single candle glints off the polished steel of Bowie's fighting knife.

It is no secret that Jim Bowie is dying. He has been sick since long before the siege began. Some say that he has been either sick or drunk since the death of his wife two years ago. Then, on February 24, he was helping to position one of the Texans' twelve-pounders when the heavy cannon broke loose and crushed his ribs.

Davy quietly sets his rifle beside the door and takes a few steps across the tiny room.

"Crockett," a weak voice groans from the cot, followed by a wild fit of coughing. Bowie, pale as death, struggles up on one elbow. "Has it started yet?"

"Nope, not yet. Reckon it will before first light, though." He slips the brace of pistols from his belt and lays them beside Bowie. "The boys thought you might like to have these."

A hollow smile spreads across Bowie's tortured face. Something like a laugh escapes him as he carefully places one pistol on each side of his knife. "Thanks, Davy. When the time comes, I'll try to put 'em to good use." Bowie coughs violently, leaving a few more drops of blood on the floor. Then he slumps back on his cot and seems to be asleep again. Davy watches him for a moment. Even in this condition, Bowie is a man to be admired.

This is Jim Bowie, perhaps the most famous knife fighter in all the world. This is the man who had killed the famous French duelist Countrecourt in a duel in New Orleans. They fought at night, in a pitch-black room without windows. This is the same man who had killed Diego Porto in a sit-down duel where both Bowie and his opponent had one leg of their pants nailed to a log.

This is the Jim Bowie who, fifteen years before, had earned the respect of the wily privateer Jean Lafitte and made a fortune with him in the slave trade. Bowie is dying of tuberculosis, yet he clings desperately to life, determined to stay alive long enough to die in battle.

Something on the stone floor beside Bowie's cot catches Davy's eye and he picks it up. It is a cameo, a tiny painting framed in gold. In the flickering candlelight, Davy sees the face of a pretty, delicate young woman with dark hair. "Bowie's wife," he whispers and lays it beside the pistols.

Jim Bowie's illness, everyone knows, has been made worse by the years of hard drinking which followed the death of his beloved Ursula. Perhaps Bowie has come to the Alamo to die. Perhaps, through all the battles and duels, he has only been looking for someone to kill him and put an end to the misery. Davy is not sure, but whatever the reasons, he will always be proud to have fought alongside Jim Bowie.

Hard experience has taught Davy that losing a wife can ruin a man. Even now, so many years later, he is not sure how he survived the death of his own wife and kept going.

Polly. Her memory is close to him and strong, dissolving the battered wall of the Alamo, calling him back to the green hills of home.

* * *

The autumn sun cast a soft golden haze over the freshly harvested fields. A cool nip was in the air, and corn shocks stood like a village of Indian tepees. Evening was not far away, and the harvest was all but completed. As was the custom in that time, folks had come from miles around to help their neighbors with the hard work of getting the crops in before winter. But there was much more to harvest time than just work.

When the last of the corn was in the crib and the wheat all thrashed, there was a great festival. It was a time for dancing, parties, games, and, of course, shooting matches. Often, it was also a time for courting.

Among those who had come to help with the harvest that fall was David Crockett. Although only nineteen years old, he had grown into a handsome young man with dark hair and dark blue eyes, a man who had earned a reputation both as a hard worker and a hard fighter. He had also become one of the best rifle shots in all of Tennessee.

Also at the harvest that year was a girl named Polly Finley. She was the daughter of Jean and William Finley, who lived some fifteen miles away and had also come to help with the harvest.

Polly was just sixteen that fall, but in those days, that was just about "marryin' age." She was a small girl with sparkling eyes and auburn hair, which hung gracefully about her shoulders. She had already heard quite a bit about David Crockett, and most of it she did not like. He was known to swear quite frequently and drink whiskey on occasion. The shooting matches and bear hunts that he spent so much time at were known to be

25

attended by a rough crowd. She suspected that he also gambled at cards.

David Crockett had heard only one thing about Polly Finley, and he doubted very much that it could be true. "Why, she's jest about the prettiest little girl you'll ever lay eyes on in all of Tennessee," a friend had told him a few weeks before.

By this point in David's life, he had had about the same luck with girls as he had with school. Twice he had been in love, and twice he had been left. His first love had been a young woman from North Carolina. She had come to visit her uncle, whom David was working for at that time. She had no intentions of marrying a poor hunter from the backwoods and soon became engaged to someone else.

David had gotten as near as the week before the wedding when he learned that his second sweetheart was secretly planning to run away with another. As the saying goes, "The fox was getting trap-shy."

He had not been at the reaping very long before he met Polly's mother. This did nothing to encourage his interest in her daughter.

"Well now, if you aren't a fine young lad there with your rosy red cheeks," she greeted him with a heavy Irish accent and pinched his cheeks until he blushed. "Sure an' it be I've got a sweetheart for you."

"Reckon she's come ta get her daughter married off," someone whispered loud enough for David to hear.

It was evening before David was at last introduced to Polly. A huge party was planned to celebrate the successful harvest. The largest barn was decorated with lanterns. A feast of roast venison and bear meat, potatoes, fresh baked bread, and apple cider was spread out on long tables. Fiddles and mandolins supplied the music as David and Polly danced to the lilting reels and the schottische. In the wee hours of the morning, they took part in several little plays for the amusement of the children who were allowed to stay up all night for such a special occasion.

By the time they parted company in the morning, David was sure that he would be seeing Miss Polly Finley again, even though she lived some fifteen miles away, which was nearly a day's walk. David immediately made a deal with a friend to purchase a horse. Since he had no money, he agreed to work six months to pay off the horse.

During the weeks that followed, David found himself thinking of little else besides Polly. After almost six weeks had passed, he could stand it no longer. On a Saturday morning he took his rifle, mounted his horse, and rode the fifteen miles to see Polly.

It was afternoon before David finally dismounted and tied his horse to the big oak tree in front of the Finley house. He was met by Polly's father, who seemed to be an agreeable man and quite friendly. Polly, he was told, was not at home. Her mother, once again very talkative, began asking David all kinds of questions about himself.

It was near evening when Polly finally arrived home in a carriage driven by a richly dressed young man about David's age. David's heart sank. He was sure he had been beaten before he even started. Polly stepped lightly from the carriage and greeted him with a smile that made his knees feel weak.

"What brings you all the way over here?" she asked.

"Reckon I come a courtin' a little too late," he answered, avoiding her eyes as he pulled off his coonskin cap.

"Well, maybe you did and maybe you didn't," Polly answered with a twinkle in her blue eyes and a teasing grin on her pretty face.

"This here is Mr. Anson Carter," Polly said, quickly changing the subject before David could say anything else.

27

The young man limply shook his hand and stared down his long aristocratic nose at David. He was plainly unimpressed with this backwoods bumpkin, all the way from the tail of his coonskin cap to the toes of his leather moccasins. David glared back at him.

"Mr. Carter here has a long drive home," Polly added, but he did not seem to take the hint.

They all retired to the front porch, and it was not long before Anson Carter found himself being ignored as Polly seated herself very close to David. Every now and then, David added to his displeasure by snarling at him like a wildcat when no one was looking. Before the evening was very old, Mr. Carter took his leave.

A full moon poked its way over the mountain peaks and hung for a while in the branches of the big oak tree. Crickets chirped beside the front porch, and fireflies blinked their friendly lights in the fields beyond.

Polly and David sat close together and talked of many things that night. David felt wonderful. He told Polly of his travels with old Jacob Siler and of learning to shoot. He told her also of whipping Angus McGruffy and then running away from home to work and travel for two more years. During that time he had journeyed to faraway Baltimore, where he had almost signed aboard a ship bound for England.

"Reckon I'm glad you didn't turn to sailin'," Polly said softly. "I might never have met you then."

"Reckon I'm glad about that too," David answered, and before he knew it, he had kissed her.

They sat quietly for a long time then, happily watching the moon rise above the trees. It was quite late when David finally said that he must start for home.

Polly smiled at him in the moonlight. "Why, David Crockett, I wouldn't hear of it. It's all of fifteen miles. You just stay here tonight. We've got plenty of room."

David stayed until Monday morning. By that time,

"*He found himself haunted by stories of new land, farther west.*"

29

he had made up his mind that he wanted Polly for his wife.

David and Polly were married on August 16, 1806. As a wedding present, Polly's parents gave them two cows and calves. Another friend gave them fifteen dollars of credit at the local store.

David rented a small farm with a cabin on it and set to farming. He probably believed that farming was what he would do for the rest of his life.

Polly proved to be a good homemaker. She was skilled with her spinning wheel and easily made clothing and blankets for the new little family.

As their first few years together passed, two sons were born to the Crocketts: John Wesley in 1807 and William in 1809. But David slowly began to realize that he was not cut out to be a farmer. He knew little about growing crops and milking cows. Even when his year's work showed a small profit, the high rent on their farm took it all and always left them deeper in debt.

David was a fine hunter, a crack shot with a rifle, as well as being skilled in reading the signs and tracks of wild animals. But the game was scarce in the forest around his rented farm. Always, he found himself haunted by stories of new land farther west, where the deer and bear were plentiful and the land free for the taking.

"I hear tell the Elk River Country is openin' up fur settlers. Injuns is settled down out there now," a neighbor told David one afternoon as he leaned against the rail fence around his cornfield. "Some say the deer are so thick out there yer liable to kill two of 'em with one shot if ya ain't careful."

David's hoe nicked another rock and sent a few sparks flying as he dug weeds. "I reckon the only thing that grows good fur me is these here weeds," he said bitterly as he leaned his hoe against a tree.

"Some folks is just natural cut out fur farmin'," the neighbor added thoughtfully. "Others just ain't."

30

David knew his neighbor was right and, in the fall of 1811, the Crocketts moved west. For David it was to be the first of many moves. It was the beginning of a restless, lifelong search, ever westward, for new land where the game was more plentiful and the grass greener.

At this time David owned one old horse and a pair of two-year-old colts. On them he packed all of his family's belongings that could be carried. Polly's father lent them one more pack horse and went along to help with the move.

The Elk River Country lay between the Elk River and the Duck River in middle Tennessee, very near the border with Alabama. Two years later, he would move his family once again. This time they settled on Bean Creek, which lies about ten miles south of the present town of Winchester. He homesteaded five acres of land there. For a while, it seemed, he was satisfied. The wild game was very plentiful. There were more bears than he had found anywhere else.

The bear was an important part of frontier life. A family could easily use six of them in a year. One fat bear would make several barrels of meat which tasted a little like pork and could be salted to last through the winter. The hides were made into blankets and coats. Bear fat made lard for cooking as well as grease for oiling guns and wagon wheels.

On Bean Creek, David hunted and farmed a little, while Polly kept the cabin clean, cooked, and made the family's clothing. If things had been only a little different, David Crockett might have remained there, peacefully hunting and farming for the rest of his life. But that was not to be. On August 13, 1813, the Creek Indians attacked Fort Mims and killed 500 men, women, and children. David Crockett went to war.

5

"What are you thinking about, Davy?" Bowie's weak voice brings Davy back to the dark realities of the Alamo.

"Not thinkin', jes' rememberin'," Davy answers.

"I guess you've got a heap of remembering to do," Bowie says. "No matter what happens here when the sun comes up, it will always be said that you lived one heck of a life."

Davy chuckles. "Reckon the same might be said about you, Jim. How many duels is it they say you fought?"

Bowie's hand touches the ivory handle of his knife. "That doesn't matter. But do you remember the way you felt the first time you went into a battle?"

"That would have been during the Creek War, the battle they come to call 'Big Bloody.' Reckon I was so scared then, I wished my pa never had met up with my ma. Joined up right after the Fort Mims massacre. Least ways in that war, we took to the woods, hunted the enemy 'till we found 'em and then fought 'em. Liked that a heap better than bein' cooped up like we are here."

* * *

Word of the massacre at Fort Mims had spread like wildfire across the Tennessee frontier. Early in September of 1813, a messenger brought the news to Crockett's homestead.

Fort Mims was located near the junction of the Tombigbee and the Alabama rivers, just north of the present town of Mobile, Alabama, and almost 300 miles south of Crockett's farm.

The fort's commander had refused to believe that an attack was coming. Even after a Negro slave twice reported seeing Indians sneaking up on the fort, he still refused to close the gates. As a result of his foolishness, over 1,000 Creek warriors stormed into the fort. Before the day was over, 500 men, women, and children had been killed.

Within a few days of hearing about the Fort Mims massacre, David had taken his best horse and had ridden to the nearby town of Winchester, where the local militia was gathering. There he joined the army as a private in a company of Tennessee Mounted Riflemen.

Almost at once they received orders to march to Bealy's Spring, a few miles south of the present town of Huntsville, Alabama. They camped there and waited as other troops began to arrive from all over the frontier. Andrew Jackson, the army's commanding general, was still several days away, marching with a large number of troops from Nashville.

Within a day or two of David's arrival, he was picked for a scouting party that spent several days across the river, inside enemy territory. They scouted the location of the main body of Creek Indians. There was no actual fighting on the patrol, but David was placed in charge of half of the men when the party divided in order to cover more ground.

General Jackson and the remainder of the army arrived shortly after the scouting party returned. The entire army marched the next morning.

There followed long days of forced marches, nights of guard duty, and little sleep as they pushed farther and farther into Indian territory. They crossed the Tennessee River, passed Huntsville, and recrossed the river again at Muscle Shoals.

Almost no provisions had arrived, and David spent most of his time hunting bear and deer to feed the troops as they marched. About the only other food they received was a cache of corn they looted from an Indian village called Black Warrior Town, which the Creeks had abandoned when they heard the army coming.

It was not until the first of November that Jackson's scouts located a large number of Creeks at an Indian town called Tallusahatchee, just up the river. This was the information that Jackson had been waiting for, and the army moved that night. David Crockett was about to get his first bitter taste of war.

The long column of silent riders snaked its way through the forest. Above them, the waning moon cast a cold, pale light through the bare branches where only a few leaves still clung. The north wind whispered, stirring the dry leaves along the trail and sounding always like footsteps in the darkness. David tightened his grip on his Kentucky rifle and eased it higher in the crook of his arm.

It was after three o'clock in the morning when his company at last dismounted and left their horses. They crept forward then, keeping close enough together to remain in a straight line until they reached the edge of a large meadow. Far in the distance they could see the glowing embers of a few cooking fires, which marked the Indians' camp.

They lay down on the ground and hid themselves as best they could. David wiggled his way down into the leaves and broke a couple of branches from in front of him to make certain that he had a clear field of fire in the direction of the camp. His hands were shaking as he laid his powderhorn and shot bag within easy reach and then drove his tomahawk into the ground beside them. One last time he checked the charge in his rifle and then tried to rest.

The trap was set. There was nothing more to do until morning. That night David Crockett learned that the worst part of a battle was the waiting before it started.

Dawn came as a pink haze beyond the trees. David watched as the Indian camp began to stir. He could see now that it was more than just a camp. There were many huts and log houses. Warm coals from the cooking fires were being stirred into flame, and soon a veil of gray smoke hung over the town and the odor of roasting meat drifted to where the army lay in ambush.

General Jackson had an excellent plan of attack. During the night, with an army of over 900 men, he had surrounded the town on three sides. Just after sunrise, Jackson sent two companies of rangers, under Captain Hammond, riding into the open in front of the town. When the Indians saw them, they immediately attacked, believing that a small group of soldiers had blundered into the town. The rangers fired a few shots and then turned to run, with the Indians screaming after them.

Nearly 200 warriors charged into the ambush. The forest around them exploded, and dozens fell in the first volley. Jackson's troops then charged into the town. The fighting was hand-to-hand, rifle butts and knives against tomahawks and war clubs.

Arrows sang in the air as David ran into the town. Suddenly, he saw in front of him an old Indian woman sitting on the steps of her house and using her feet to draw back a bow. Before David could react, her arrow sailed passed his ear and buried into the chest of a lieutenant only a few feet away. It was his first time to see a man killed with an arrow. He would never forget it. By the time he looked away, the Indian woman was dead from the blasts of about twenty rifle balls.

Some of the warriors surrendered, but others refused and began to retreat into one of the large buildings where they continued to fire back with bows and rifles. Troops quickly surrounded them and, while a steady rain of rifle balls poured into the house, other men crept up and set it on fire. Still, these Creek warriors refused to surrender and they fought to the last man.

Forty-six warriors died inside the burning house that morning, bringing the Indian losses to 186 killed and 80 taken prisoner. Jackson's army had lost only five men, but the horrors of "Big Bloody" were only beginning.

The men had still not received any food supplies, and for several days now they had been on half-rations. On the day after the battle, it was learned that there was a cellar full of potatoes under the house where the last of the Creek warriors had burned to death.

David was sent back with a party of men to dig into the burned-out house and recover the potatoes. To do so, they had to drag out many of the half-burned bodies. The cellar was there and the potatoes proved to be edible. In fact, they were already cooked.

Long marches and more bloody battles would follow. Talladega, Horseshoe Bend, and then a long series of dangerous search-and-destroy missions against small bands of Creeks still holding out in the swamps of southern Alabama and northern Florida. When it was finally over, David had seen enough fighting to last him a lifetime.

Two things happened to him during the Creek War which would affect his later life. David developed a strong dislike for his commanding officer, Gen. Andrew Jackson, and for professional soldiers in general. He also developed a healthy respect for the Indian. Years later, as a United States congressman, he would bitterly oppose President Andrew Jackson over the question of Indian rights and Indian lands.

6

Bowie moves on his cot. Slowly, his eyes focus on Davy as he leans against the baptistery wall. Bowie's hand brushes the cameo lying beside his knife and pistols. He picks it up.

"Your wife?" Davy asks quietly.

Bowie nods as he stares at the picture. "Ursula." He pauses for a long moment. "She died of the cholera two years back. Guess I've been tryin' to find some way to die myself ever since."

"Losin' a wife is jest about the hardest trial which ever befalls a man. When my Polly died two years after the Creek War, reckon I felt about the same way."

"You had the good sense to marry again."

"Had to," Davy answers. "Had me two sons and a daughter by then and I found out real fast I weren't much account fur being a mother and a father both."

Polly. For a moment her memory floats again before him and then fades. Instead he sees the rough mound of gray fieldstones which mark her lonely grave behind his cabin in Tennessee. Wildflowers bloom like a patchwork quilt on the hillside around it, and birds sing in the trees. Davy hopes that her spirit has peace.

Polly Crockett died in the spring of 1815. That was shortly after the birth of their third child, a girl they named Margaret.

A year later David married Elizabeth Patton, a widow of about his age whose husband had been killed in the Creek War. She was a large woman who had both a son and a daughter of her own. She was also intelligent, practical, and seems to have been much better at handling the business of farming than David had ever been. It was to become a good and practical marriage.

The ceremony took place on a warm Sunday afternoon in the living room of the Patton home. The guests had come from far and wide and were dressed in their Sunday best. Moments before the bride was to make her appearance, one of the family pigs wandered in through the open front door. The old boar hog gave the guests a long look, then grunted and began rooting around under the furniture. Needless to say, there was considerable laughter and the ceremony was in danger of being totally disrupted.

David rose solemnly and, with much ceremony, escorted the pig back outside. "From now on, Ol' Hook, I'll do all the gruntin' around here," he said, to the amusement of all those present.

Within a few months of the wedding, David was again headed west, looking for "more elbow room." Accompanied by three of his neighbors, he crossed the Tennessee River at Ditto's Landing and headed into what had been Creek territory before the war. David had liked the country he had seen during the war. Now that it was open for settlement, he decided to have a good look at it. His little party of adventurers reached the Black Warrior River and followed it downstream through Jones Valley.

They camped one night not far from the old Black Warrior Town, near where David had fought in the battle of "Big Bloody." Almost as if the spirits of the dead Creek warriors were unhappy with their presence, things began to go wrong.

During the night, their horses somehow broke loose and wandered off. David began tracking them in the morning and traveled all day on foot. By evening he had still not caught up with them. Much worse than that, David also had to admit that he was becoming very sick, perhaps for the first time in his life.

He spent the night at the cabin of one the area's few settlers and, although he felt no better in the morning, he started out again to try to get back to where his companions were waiting for him. Before he reached them, he became too weak to continue. He lay down beside the trail and wondered if he was going to die.

Two friendly Indians found him sometime that afternoon and did nothing to make him feel any better. They examined him and then spoke to him in sign language, telling him that he would surely die very soon. "This," David thought, "was a thing I was confoundedly afraid of myself!"

The Indians helped him to the nearest house, which was about a mile and a half away. He was still alive the next day, when two of his companions happened along on foot and took him with them as far as the house of Jesse Jones, one of the area's earliest settlers. David's companions bought new horses there and prepared to start back for Tennessee. It was obvious that David was in no condition to travel any farther. He stayed with the Joneses for another two weeks before traveling home himself.

News on the frontier had a way of getting mixed up sometimes. David's companions left him at the Joneses' cabin and returned to Tennessee. They were so certain that he was going to die that by the time they told the story to Elizabeth, they swore that he was already dead!

"We left him dying and later we talked to men who had seen him draw his last breath and helped to bury him," they insisted.

David would later write about the reports of his death by saying only, "I know'd this was a whopper of a lie, as soon as I heard it."

A year later, David started out again to explore new land. This time he got only as far as Shoal Creek, about eighty miles away. Again he found himself sick with fever. Judging from the symptoms, he was probably again suffering from malaria. This time the attack was not so bad and he recovered in a short time.

While he was getting over this round of sickness, he took time to have a good look around the area of Shoal Creek. He liked it so much that he decided to settle there. Within another year, he had built a cabin at the head of Shoal Creek, cleared a field, planted corn, and moved his family there.

"It was here," he wrote later, "that I begun to take a rise." It was here that he first got into politics.

There was no law on the newly opened areas of the Tennessee frontier. Another two years passed before David and his neighbors decided that any laws were needed at all. By this time there were quite a few outlaws and other undesirable types moving into the area. A meeting was held and, much to his own surprise, David found himself elected to be a magistrate.

"Why, I ain't never read one page in a law book in all my life!" David protested when the votes were counted.

"Don't matter none out here," he was told. "Ye got good common horse sense an' that's what counts, far as we're concerned."

So David agreed to take on the job of magistrate. For over a year, his word was law in the country around Shoal Creek. The job of a magistrate on the frontier was not easy. There were no written laws, and justice was expected to be dealt out solely on the basis of honesty and common sense.

At this time, David could barely write his name and could not have read a law book if he had had one. Despite this, he quickly gained a reputation for fairness and honesty.

Sometimes his methods were a little different. "When a man owed a debt and wouldn't pay it, I would give judgement against him and then an order of an execution would easily scare the debt out of him," David admitted in later years.

When Shoal Creek officially became part of Lawrence County, Tennessee, David continued on as magistrate. He even managed to improve his handwriting enough to write his own arrest warrants and keep his record book.

It was also during this time that David's military career "began to take a rise." Every state then was expected to keep a militia. This was a kind of forerunner of today's National Guard. Each county had one regiment, and it was the custom of the time for the men to elect their own commander.

One day, in 1818, David was approached by Captain Matthews, who was one of the area's most prosperous farmers and an officer in the local militia. Matthews said that he was going to run for election as colonel of the Lawrence County Regiment. He asked David to run for the position of first major.

David at first refused. Bitter memories of the Creek War still haunted him. He told Matthews, "I reckon I done my share of fighting." But Captain Matthews insisted over and over again until David finally agreed to run.

Matthews invited him to come to a cornhusking and "frolic" he was holding at his farm in order to get people to vote for him. Shortly after David and his family arrived, he was told that Matthews's son was running for the same position as David and that Matthews was, of course, supporting his son. This bit of information "got David's dander up." He called Captain Matthews aside and demanded an explanation.

The older man admitted the truth and said, "My son hates worse to run against you than any man in the county."

David thought for a moment and then answered, "Your son need give himself no uneasiness about that. I won't run against him for major. I'm running against his daddy fur colonel!"

When the election was over, both Captain Matthews and his son were badly beaten, and David Crockett had earned the title of colonel.

Perhaps David Crockett believed once again that this is where he would remain, living out his life hunting, farming, and doing his part to maintain law and order in Lawrence County, Tennessee. But before the year of 1818 was finished, David would be asked to run for the state legislature. His decision to "go ahead" would launch him on a new and awesome career. Had history been only a little bit different, had fate been only a bit kinder, it was a career which might well have taken him all the way to the presidency of the United States.

7

Jim Bowie is again unconscious as Davy leaves the baptistery. The figure of a woman moves in the shadows inside the roofless chapel. Davy recognizes her as Susanna Dickinson, the wife of Capt. Almeron Dickinson. She came in with her husband and the thirty-two volunteers from Gonzales. Several days ago, when Santa Anna allowed the women and children to leave the Alamo, Susanna refused to go. In her arms is a child, although she is little more than a child herself.

"Colonel Crockett?" she asks in a shaky voice, "will it begin soon?"

Davy looks up at the night sky. The stars seem a bit paler now. "Reckon it might do jest that about anytime now. You best be takin' little Angelina into one of the side rooms there. That'll be the safest place."

Light from a nearby fire reflects against her hair as she turns to go and then hesitates. "I bet you wish you were back in Washington City, speaking in the halls of Congress," she says, mustering a bit of a smile.

Davy scratches his head. "Well, ma'am, as I remember it, there was usually a fight of some kind goin' on there too. Least ways, there was a heap of back-stabbin' come election time."

Susanna Dickinson vanishes into the shadows. For a moment Davy is alone, standing before the tall wooden doors of the Alamo's chapel. They remind him of similar doors he once walked through to make his first speech as a congressman of the United States. He had been almost as scared then as he is now, in these last minutes before battle.

* * *

"The chair recognizes the honorable David Crockett, congressman from the great state of Tennessee," the Speaker's voice announced. His gavel rang through the halls of Congress.

A murmur of laughter rippled through the crowd as David rose slowly to his feet. The congressman from Tennessee was dressed in a buckskin hunting shirt, buckskin trousers, and moccasins. He removed his coonskin cap and laid it on his desk.

His speech was like none which had ever been heard in Congress. It would become an important part of the legend of Davy Crockett.

"They tell me that every new congressman is supposed to make a speech of introduction," David's strong voice boomed from the floor of the Senate chambers. "Well, I got one jest bustin' ta get out, so here goes.

"I'm Davy Crockett, fresh from the backwoods. I'm half horse, half alligator, with jes' a touch of snappin' turtle. I'm a screamer and ring-tailed roarer. I got the fastest horse, the prettiest sister, the surest rifle, and the ugliest dog in Tennessee. My father can lick any man in Kentucky and I can lick my father . . ."

The unlikely rise of David Crockett from backwoods magistrate to United States congressman had begun in 1820, when he agreed to run for the Tennessee legislature. Just as he had known nothing about the law when

44

he became a magistrate, he knew even less about politics when he first ran for political office.

In those days, political gatherings were held quite often to allow the various candidates to meet and debate the important issues. These gatherings were usually held along with a "frolic," a barbeque, a hunt, or just about any other excuse to get together and have a good time.

The first of these gatherings that David attended was at a squirrel hunt. He had never made a public speech in his life, and he knew nothing of the issues that the candidates were debating. There were several candidates scheduled to speak that day, and David was to be second. He hoped that, by listening to one of his opponents, he would have time to learn something about speechmaking before his turn came. But, as the man's long-winded oration dragged on and on, David could see that the crowd was becoming very tired.

When it was at last his turn, he told the crowd that he didn't think there was much of a speech in him anyway and, since he was "dry as a powder horn," he thought he would go over to the whiskey barrel and wet his whistle. The crowd applauded and quickly followed him, leaving the other opponents with no one to listen to them.

Meanwhile, David told stories about bear hunting and Indian fighting to the delight of all. In fact, it worked so well that it was to become a trademark of his whole political career. When the campaign was over and the votes were counted, David had received more than twice as many votes as his opponent. He became a representative to the Tennessee state legislature.

David served two successful terms in the Tennessee legislature. As always, he developed a reputation for fairness and honesty, which made him a hero of the working people throughout the frontier.

As his second term drew to a close in 1825, David was urged to run for the national Congress. Although he was defeated in his first attempt, he ran again in 1827.

In this campaign he was pitted against two powerful and experienced opponents. There was Col. Adam Alexander, who had already served one term in Congress. Challenging him was William Arnold, a lawyer and city commissioner, as well as a major general in the militia. Neither of these men considered David Crockett to be any threat to their campaign.

They decided that the best way to handle Crockett was to ignore him. At every debate they argued with each other but were careful never to say anything to or about him. They believed that by doing this, they would convince the voters that Crockett knew nothing about the issues and could not be considered a serious candidate.

David showed them otherwise. At one big gathering, he spoke first and kept his speech short and to the point. Colonel Alexander spoke next and talked about many of the same things David had said but acted like he was not even there. When it was General Arnold's turn to speak, he replied only to Alexander's comments.

Arnold's speech was almost half over when a flock of guinea-fowl wandered up close to the speaker's platform and began making such a noise that they interrupted the speech. Arnold insisted that the guineas be driven off so he could finish his speech.

As soon as Arnold was finished, David got to his feet and approached General Arnold. "Well, general, you are the first man I ever saw that understood the language of guinea-fowls."

The general looked confused and the crowd went completely silent. "Since you did not have the politeness to name me in your speech, and when my little friends came up and began to holler 'Crockett, Crockett, Crockett,' you had them all driven away." The crowd laughed loudly and the story spread far and wide. When it was all over, David Crockett became Congressman Crockett.

When David arrived in Washington in December of 1827, the presidential term of John Adams was almost over. Gen. Andrew Jackson, David's former commanding officer from the Creek War, was campaigning heavily. "Old Hickory," as he was commonly called, was elected the following year.

David had never liked Jackson and, likewise, Jackson had no love for David Crockett. There could be no doubt that, sooner or later, the two would clash bitterly. Despite this, David seems to have supported Jackson at first. Then slowly he became angered and discouraged with all the corrupt and crooked dealings he saw in Jackson's administration.

From the very beginning, David pushed for the passage of a land bill that would allow the poor people living along the Tennessee frontier to buy vacant public land cheaply. Many other politicians from Tennessee opposed this idea. Instead they wanted to sell the vacant lands in their state at the best prices they could get. David believed that this would drive many penniless pioneers off the land which they had worked so hard to settle.

The land bill David wanted was never passed during his lifetime. It was his son, John Wesley, who followed in his father's footsteps and was elected to Congress in 1839, who succeeded in getting the bill passed in 1841.

David also argued against using government money to support the military academy at West Point. He felt that only sons of rich and important families attended West Point and that poor people should not have to help pay for the education of the rich. He was not entirely correct, as a number of young men without money began very successful army careers at West Point.

He also opposed West Point because he felt that officers who had graduated from it would enjoy many special privileges. On this point he was probably correct. Even today, it is very unusual for an officer to rise to

47

the rank of general in the United States Army without having graduated from West Point.

Although many of the bills he supported were never passed, David's reputation continued to grow. It was probably about this time that he began to be called "Davy" instead of David. Davy Crockett became known as "an honest politician," and many people went to Washington just to get a glimpse of him.

He tried to find a little time for everyone who wanted his company. Newspaper reporters loved to write about him and quote his backwoods jokes and tall tales. His wit and wisdom were compared to Benjamin Franklin, and it was only natural that people began to talk of Crockett for president.

8

The shrill blast of a bugle shatters the silence as Davy watches Susanna Dickinson disappear into one of the chapel's siderooms.

From somewhere in the darkness, Travis is yelling, "Come on men, the Mexicans are upon us!"

Gripping his rifle in front of him, Davy runs for his position on the south wall. Already he can hear the distant drumming of thousands of pairs of feet as the Mexican infantry runs on the hard ground outside the walls.

At last, it begins.

Rifles are firing all around him as Davy throws himself against the wall, poking his rifle barrel out at the mass of charging shadows before him. He squeezes his trigger. Old Betsy jumps in his hands. It is too dark to see if his ball has found a mark. As he jerks the plug out of his powder horn and dumps a charge down the barrel, he is sure that his first shot was not wasted. With so many targets, it would have been hard to miss.

He rams home another ball and dumps more powder into the priming pan. The Mexicans are screaming as they charge the walls. Their battle cries rise like a howling wind in the night. From across the compound, the

Texans' bull-throated eighteen-pounder roars out in answer, cutting down a dozen soldiers carrying scaling ladders.

Above it all, Santa Anna's regimental band is playing the "Deguello," a Moorish battle march with high, blood-curdling bugle notes. Deguello, which means "slit the throat," is the signal that no prisoners will be taken— everyone is to be killed.

Davy fires again. This time his target is an officer with a sword raised in one hand and a pistol in the other. He is very close. His body falls forward against the wall and hangs there among the sharpened wooden stakes which form its top.

The battle becomes a dizzy haze of ram, prime, and fire, ram, prime, and fire, repeated over and over again as fast as Davy can perform the long-practiced exercise. Around him the noise is deafening. Cannons on either side are thundering, and foul-smelling smoke rolls over him with each round. The air is alive with screaming musket balls.

But in the darkness beyond the walls, there is confusion growing among the attackers. Their casualties are far greater than expected, and they begin falling back, trying desperately to regroup.

A cheer rises from the Alamo walls as the Texans see the attack begin to fail. The sound rings in Davy's ears like the cheering of the crowds that welcomed him to so many eastern cities in those distant days when his fame was growing in Washington.

They had cheered when he made speeches in Congress. They had cheered when he told his tall tales of bear hunts and Indian fights. There were cheers when he entered the theater to see a play that many said had been written in his honor. But when they cheered him that night, just as the Texans were cheering now, it was for a victory which could never be won.

* * *

The house lights at Washington Theater were warm and bright that winter evening in 1833. Crystal chandeliers sparkled like thousands of diamonds suspended from the towering, gilded ceiling, and the massive velvet curtains were still drawn across the stage. A hush fell over the crowd and every head turned toward the isle as Congressman David Crockett was escorted down the aisle.

A sudden roar of applause swept through the theater, resounding again and again as the crowd rose to their feet. David waved to them and bowed slightly as he took his seat in the center section of the fourth row. The house lights dimmed and the crowd took their seats. Whispers of "that's Davy Crockett; he is going to be our next president," rippled among the audience.

David settled himself comfortably in his seat and looked at the printed program in his hand: "The Lion of the West, a play in three acts by James Kirke Pauling."

The curtains were drawn back in a rush of velvet, revealing a painted scene which could well have been David's own beloved Tennessee hills. Onto the stage stepped a figure dressed in buckskins and a hat made from the skin of a wildcat. Shifting the long rifle in his hand, he swaggered to center stage and howled like a wolf. "I'm Colonel Nimrod Wildfire. I'm half horse, half alligator with jes' a little bit of snappin' turtle, I got the fastest horse, the ugliest dog, the prettiest sister—." Almost word for word, it was David's opening speech to Congress, and the crowd loved it.

A strange and unpleasant feeling swept over David. The character on the stage was so much like himself; or, more correctly, it was the image of Davy Crockett that David had helped to build himself. It was as if he was seeing a cartoon character of himself with all of his features made larger than life. His speech, his dress, even the way he walked—it was all the same, yet different.

The legendary figure of Davy Crockett had come to life to meet his maker.

"It's like I'm meetin' myself comin' back," David whispered.

David was now in his third term in Congress. Andrew Jackson's last term as president of the United States would be over in two years. Everywhere people were wondering who would follow Old Hickory to the highest office in the land. Many said that it would be Davy Crockett.

The Whig Party, as the Republicans were called at that time, believed that David might be the right man to be their candidate. To find out just how popular he was, they arranged a tour of the major eastern cities to help drum up support.

David left Washington in April of 1834 and traveled as far as Baltimore. The next day he crossed the Chesapeake River on a steamboat and traveled the remaining seventeen miles to Philadelphia on the newest form of transportation in the world—a railroad train.

"Hold onto your hat, Congressman Crockett," David was advised as he approached the newfangled machine. "And watch out for burning cinders coming from the smoke stack, they'll set ya afire sometimes."

David gave the long metal monster a serious look before he climbed aboard. The locomotive had a shiny black iron boiler with copper bands around it. On the rear was a little platform where the engineer stood at the controls. Steam was hissing from cylinders near the huge driving wheels, and the odor of wood smoke mingled with that of oil and grease.

Coupled to the locomotive was a flat car, which was piled high with wood for fuel. The rest of the train was made up of three coaches, which looked very much like horse-drawn stagecoaches hooked together. Their special wheels were designed to keep them on the tracks.

David ducked his head as he climbed into one of the coaches and seated himself against the plush velvet of the padded bench inside. "It's been said that this train has reached speeds of over twenty miles an hour," one of his companions said doubtfully.

"Why, that'd be faster than most steamboats running downriver," David answered. Actually, the train managed to reach a speed of just over eighteen miles an hour that day. Still, David had to look at his watch twice to believe that they had arrived in Philadelphia in just under one hour.

In Philadelphia, David was greeted by huge crowds of cheering people who wanted to "shake the hand of an honest politician." David was treated as he had never been treated before. He rode in the finest carriages and stayed in the finest hotels. In Philadelphia, as in all of the cities which followed, there was a constant round of speechmaking and fancy dinners. There were also tours of new factories and old battle sites.

In Boston he visited Bunker Hill, where one of the early battles of the American Revolution had been fought almost fifty years earlier. He was deeply touched and later wrote: "I felt like calling them [the patriot soldiers] up, and asking them to tell me how to help protect the liberty they bought for us with their blood; but as I could not do so, I resolved, on that holy ground, to go for my country, always and everywhere."

He was again in Philadelphia, nearing the end of his tour, when he received what he considered the finest present of his entire life, a custom-built rifle he would call "Pretty Betsy." It was one of the newer percussion-lock rifles that did not depend on a spark from a piece of flint rock to fire. Instead it used a small brass cap which fired a spark into the gunpowder inside the barrel. On the barrel was engraved in silver, "From the Young Whigs of Philadelphia."

The presentation was made at a dinner in his honor on the third of July. David promised to use the rifle "in

53

the defense of the nation, if need be, and to pass it on to his sons for the same purpose."

His tour ended at last in Philadelphia on Independence Day with a final round of speechmaking and dinners. By then there seemed to be little doubt in the minds of the Whig Party that Col. Davy Crockett, congressman from Tennessee and hero of the Creek Indian War, was going to be the next president of the United States.

As David boarded the steamboat that would take him downriver on the first leg of the long trip back to his home in Tennessee, he gave that same subject much thought. For a long time now, his motto had been, "Be sure you're right, then go ahead." Somehow, this time he could not be sure that he was right.

9

There is a trace of dawn in the eastern sky as Colonel Travis's cannons on the north wall bellow out a new barrage of grapeshot. Their muzzle flashes light the blood-soaked scene as powder smoke rolls in billowing storm clouds across the walls.

The second Mexican attack has begun less than ten minutes after the first has failed. Hordes of dark shadows come screaming at the south wall. All four cannons along the south wall fire at the same time. A hail of musket fire follows, and the attack begins to falter. Here and there Mexican soldiers are throwing down their rifles and screaming *"Diablos, Diablos!"*

As the attack against the south wall breaks down, Davy sees the soldiers begin swinging around toward the north to reinforce the attack there.

"Let's give Colonel Travis some help, boys!" he shouts and calls for half of his men to follow.

Now the fighting is concentrated against the north wall, where the Mexican artillery has already broken a hole. As Davy and his men arrive, a few Mexican soldiers with boarding ladders are trying to scale the wall. A dark head appears suddenly over the wall and David swings his rifle butt. With a hollow thud, the man falls backward and onto the soldiers below.

One by one the Mexican soldiers are killed as they reach the top of their ladders. Then the ladders are thrown back down to the ground, often killing the men below.

A wild cheer rises from the Alamo as the second assault fails and the Mexicans scatter for cover, leaving behind their dead and wounded. Davy cheers with them, holding his rifle high and waving his coonskin cap above his head. He feels that he must do this. The men expect it of him. He must encourage them and not show his own doubts. But deep inside, he knows that the battle is far from won.

"One more time," he tells himself. "If we can hold 'em one more time, we just might have a chance." The words have an ominous ring.

"One more time. If I had been elected to Congress just one more time," he thinks bitterly, "I might have been president of the United States in another year."

* * *

Politics was a fickle creature for Davy Crockett in the 1835 campaign. Although the Whig Party had supported him wholeheartedly just one year before, they began to wonder if they were making the right choice.

It was whispered in smoke-filled rooms and at fancy dinner parties in Washington that Davy Crockett was too hard to control. No matter how much money one group or another might contribute to his campaign, he refused to support anything in which he did not personally believe.

The Whigs needed a candidate who was well known and liked by the voters, it was true, but they also wanted someone who would do whatever they told him. In short, the whole problem seemed to be that Davy Crockett was just too honest to be considered as a presidential candidate.

For all his years in Congress, Davy had never really learned to understand the back-room deals and decisions which were part of national politics. He entered the 1835 campaign confident of the support of the Whigs who had sent him on his great speaking tour to the eastern cities and had presented him with his beautiful rifle.

It was a bitter and hard-fought campaign. Davy found himself being accused of not attending the required number of legislative sessions. His opponent charged that he had not done the job he had been hired to do and should pay back part of his salary.

Davy fought hard during the long campaign, but when the votes were finally counted, he had lost by a mere 230 votes. He went home a tired and disappointed man, discouraged with all of the double-dealing and back-stabbing which had ended his political career. Again the forests and rivers were calling to him. He longed to explore over the next hill and cross the next river.

He made one last speech in which he told the voters where they could go, and he ended by saying, "I'm going to Texas."

The territory of Texas was at that time owned by Mexico, although it was being settled mostly by people from the United States. For Davy, this new land offered many things. First of all, it offered a place to start over. He had, by this time, a long history of business failures, which had left him badly in debt. During his first term in the Tennessee legislature, he and Elizabeth had built a family business that included a grist mill, a powder mill, and a distillery on the banks of Shoal Creek. A flood had swept it all away in the spring of 1794, and the Crockett family lost over $3,000.

Even after his later move to the Obion River country in 1822, he seems always to have been in debt and struggling to survive. It was there that he spent considerable time and money building two flatboats and loading them with barrel staves (short lengths of hardwood

57

used to make barrels and kegs). He and several other men attempted to float the flatboats down the Mississippi to New Orleans, where the staves could be sold for a good profit. But as Davy's luck in business would have it, the flatboats were wrecked on a snag and the cargo was lost. Davy almost drowned, and he had to borrow money just to get back home.

He may have also believed that in Texas there was a chance he could begin a new political career as well. Rumors were already spreading that the territory might soon become either an independent republic or a new state. When and if this happened, they just might need a congressman or two.

Halley's Comet was a white streak in the night skies when Davy set out for Texas on the first day of November in 1835. Perhaps he took it as a sign and followed it west. With him were three of his neighbors, William Patton, Abner Burgin, and Lindsey K. Tinkle.

Together they followed the Mississippi River south to the mouth of the Arkansas River and entered Arkansas. They passed through the settlement of Little Rock and then on to the Red River, reaching it near the present-day city of Fulton.

By early January, they were in San Augustine, Texas, where Tinkle and Burgin turned back for their homes in Tennessee. Davy and William Patton signed the oath of allegiance to Texas, which would allow them to vote and to run for political office.

Talk of revolution was everywhere in Texas. Gen. Sam Houston, whom Davy had once met during the Creek War, was raising an army near Washington-on-the-Brazos. Farther away, at San Antonio de Bexar, Jim Bowie had just led a handful of men in an attack which drove a strong force of Mexican soldiers under General Cos out of Texas and back into Mexico. It was also said the Mexican general, Santa Anna, was marching north with an army.

58

Davy knew that it would be a fight he would have to join. Fifteen other men, most of them from Tennessee, joined Davy and called themselves the Tennessee Mounted Volunteers. With Davy as their commander, they rode west. This time he was sure that he was right, and he went ahead—all the way to San Antonio and the Alamo.

10

All along the south wall, Davy and his Tennessee boys are firing as fast as they can reload. No longer is there any need to take careful aim, for there are so many Mexican targets that it has become impossible to miss. Their uniforms of blue and red, with white crossbelts and tall hats that shine with metallic trim, blend together into a rolling sea of men as they surge against the walls like a floodtide against a castle of sand. Yet, for a few more fleeting moments, it looks as if the Texans might hold.

But the main force of this third attack is not against the south wall where Davy and his men are fighting. It has been concentrated on the north wall, where the Mexican artillery has broken down a small area. Again, the chilling notes of the "Deguello" wail above the slaughter as the first blood-red streaks of dawn stain the eastern sky.

Davy turns to see Colonel Travis standing beside his cannon on the north wall. One moment he is there, standing proud against the surging tide as he directs the fire of the eighteen-pounder. Then he falls backward, dead from a single musket ball in his head.

Mexican soldiers are pouring through the breach in the north wall as Davy turns his men to face this new threat. A musket ball sings past him and strikes the bearded man in a calico shirt beside him. He tumbles to the ground and lies in a growing pool of blood.

Davy fires at a running soldier and drops him. Without slowing down, he bites the plug out of the end of his powder horn and dumps more powder down Old Betsy's muzzle. Reaching into his shot pouch for another ball, his fingers find only one. He removes it grimly and drops it down the barrel. His last shot takes the life of a screaming Mexican officer who falls and is trampled by a dozen of his own men.

Men are dying all around him. Some are old friends, men who fought the Creek Indians and hunted bear with him in Tennessee. There are others he has met only recently in Arkansas, at Washington-on-the-Brazos or in Nacogdoches, where he signed the oath of allegiance to defend the Republic of Texas. They are all friends, all men he is proud to have known.

From out of nowhere a faceless shadow comes at him. Davy grabs Old Betsy by the barrel and swings it like a club, knocking the man senseless. Suddenly, Davy knows he has been hit. He feels nothing, but his right arm refuses to move. He is surprised to see the sleeve of his buckskin shirt torn to shreds and blood running into the palm of his hand.

Still, there is no pain. With his left hand he grips the barrel of Old Betsy although the stock is now broken. With failing strength, he swings at a soldier who has just bayoneted a wounded Texan. His blow connects and he sidesteps another bayonet. The Mexicans are everywhere. In the distance he catches a glimpse of them swarming onto the chapel roof where the tattered Texas flag is still flying.

Inches in front of him, a Mexican sergeant dies as

"For a few more fleeting moments, it looks as if the Texans
might hold."

one of the few Tennesseans who is still alive sinks a Bowie knife into his stomach.

Dawn blazes in the east. The first rays of golden sunlight reflect off the bright helmets and shiny lances of Mexican cavalry troopers as they jump their horses through the breach in the north wall to join the slaughter.

A handful of Davy's Tennesseans are still standing back-to-back in the courtyard and fighting with Bowie knives and tomahawks. "Fight your way to the Long Barracks!" Davy calls to them over the curses of the soldiers and the screams of the countless wounded and dying. There is still one more place to fight a little longer, to make the Mexicans pay with a few more lives. The barracks have been fortified with barricades at every doorway. If just a few of the men can reach them, they may be able to fight on and buy a few more precious seconds of life.

*　*　*

The sun had barely risen above the chapel roof as General Santa Anna picked his way carefully among the tangle of corpses which covered the Alamo courtyard between the south wall and the chapel doors. His uniform was spotless white with a blue sash, and a gold-handled sword hung untouched at his side. Plumes of red, white, and green swayed in the wind from atop his high, gold-trimmed, bicorn hat. He had already found it was impossible to keep the blood-soaked ground from leaving dark stains on his newly polished boots.

Although he saw no sign of any living enemy, the slaughter was still going on. Their losses had been so terrible that his soldiers seemed unable to realize that it was over, that victory was theirs. With hate-crazed eyes, they continued to shoot the dead bodies and to hack them to pieces with their swords.

The general glimpsed at Bowie's body being carried out of the baptistery, held aloft on the points of a half-dozen bayonets. As he passed, one of the soldiers cursed Bowie, saying that he killed two men with his pistols and slit the throat of a third before he died.

Santa Anna ignored the bloody orgy going on all around him. "It is a small thing," he remarked to his personal secretary.

General Castrillon, one of four Mexican field commanders, approached Santa Anna and saluted. "My general," he began, "I have taken six prisoners. What shall I do with them?"

Santa Anna glared at the officer. His frowning face turned a deep red and he shook with rage. "Have I not told you that there would be no prisoners taken?" he roared.

"My general," Castrillon protested, "they fought bravely and I have given them my word that they would not be killed."

"Then you have disobeyed my orders," Santa Anna growled.

The general's interpreter, a small man with tiny glasses, moved close to Santa Anna and touched his sleeve. "That one," he whispered, "the old one with the wounded arm, he is Davy Crockett. I met him once in Washington while he was a United States congressman."

Santa Anna turned slowly and looked into the fierce dark-blue eyes of the battered man before him. He was blackened from powder smoke and grime. His ragged buckskins were torn and burnt. A bloody gash was across his forehead. His right arm hung limp at his side, and blood had soaked what was left of his sleeve. On his graying head was a coonskin cap.

For a long, silent moment, each met the other's eyes. Then Santa Anna looked away. "Kill them," he ordered. "Kill them all!"

General Castrillon was shocked by the order. He turned his back and walked away. Several other officers followed. "Kill them!" Santa Anna shrieked again, but there was no need to repeat the order. The one they called Crockett was coming toward him, a Bowie knife clutched in his left hand and death in his eyes. Santa Anna stepped backward as a dozen muskets fired around him.

As the smoke cleared, Santa Anna took one more look at the last of the Alamo's defenders to die. Davy Crockett still gripped the Bowie knife, and his coonskin cap lay beside him in the dirt.

Some Facts About Davy Crockett

There are many versions of Crockett's death. Only recently has it been revealed that he most probably did not die during the actual battle but was executed shortly afterward. The account I have used in this book was taken from an interview made by a correspondent for a New York newspaper with a Mexican soldier captured at San Jacinto and being held on Galveston Island on June 9, 1836. There are at least eight eyewitness reports that say Crockett was alive after the battle ended and was executed along with several others. It is interesting to note that nowhere in any of these accounts is it said that Crockett surrendered. At the time of this printing, Dan Kilgore has done what I consider the best book dealing with this subject. It is entitled *How Did Davy Die?* (Texas A&M University Press, 1973).

Davy Crockett named the rifle he took to Texas and used during the battle of the Alamo, "Old Betsy." According to the official publication of the Alamo Long Barrack Museum, compiled by the Daughters of the Republic of Texas, this rifle is on display at the Alamo in San Antonio, Texas. It is inscribed "presented to David Crockett by the people of Nashville, Tennessee on May 5, 1822." This weapon was originally a flint lock which was shortened and converted to percussion lock in 1886.

"Pretty Betsy" was the name David gave to the rifle presented to him by the Whig Party in Philadelphia at the end of his famous speaking tour. It is engraved with the inscription: "Presented by the Young Whigs of Philadelphia to the honorable David Crockett." David chose not to take this rifle to Texas with him, perhaps because it was a percussion-lock weapon and required percussion caps to fire, which may not have been readily available in Texas at that time.

This weapon was located after a long search by author James Wakefield Burke and is pictured in his book *David Crockett, The Man Behind the Myth*. It is presently in the possession of a descendant of Crockett.

66

BIBLIOGRAPHY

BOOKS

Burke, James Wakefield. *David Crockett: The Man Behind the Myth*. Austin: Eakin Press, 1984.

Crockett, David. *A Narrative of the Life of David Crockett*. Philadelphia, 1834.

De La Pena, Jose Enrique. *With Santa Anna in Texas, A Personal Narrative of the Revolution*. Trans. and ed. by Carmen Perry. College Station, TX, 1975.

Driskill, Frank A. *Davy Crockett: The Untold Story*. Austin: Eakin Press, 1981.

Fritz, Jean. *Make Way for Sam Houston*. New York: Putnam, 1986.

Hauck, Richard Boyd. *Davy Crockett: A Handbook*. University of Nebraska Press, 1982.

Haythornthwaite, Philip, and Paul Hannon. *The Alamo and the War for Texas Independence 1835–36*. Osprey Men-At-Arms series #173, London: Osprey Publishing, 1986.

Holbrook, Stewart H. *Davy Crockett*. New York: Random House, 1955.

Kerr, Rita. *The Immortal 32*. Austin: Eakin Press, 1986.

Kilgore, Dan. *How Did Davy Die?* College Station: Texas A&M University Press, 1973.

Lee, Tammie. *Texas Wildflower*. New York: Zebra, 1983.

Rourke, Constance. *Davy Crockett*. New York: Harcourt, Brace & World Inc., 1934.

Shackford, James A. *David Crockett: The Man and the Legend*. Chapel Hill, NC: University of North Carolina Press, 1956.

Shackford, James A & Folmsbee, Stanley J. *A Narrative of the Life of David Crockett of the State of Tennessee*. Knoxville: University of Tennessee Press, 1973.

Tinkle, Lon. *13 Days To Glory*. New York: Signet, 1958.

Townsend, Tom. *Texas Treasure Coast*. Austin: Eakin Press, 1979.

Wellman, Paul. *The Iron Mistress*. New York: Doubleday & Company, Inc., 1951.

FILMS

Walt Disney Productions. Initial television series *Davy Crockett, Indian Fighter*, 1954. *Davy Crockett Goes To Congress*, 1955. *Davy Crockett at the Alamo*, 1955. With Fess Parker and Buddy Ebsen starring, Bill Walsh producer.

Walt Disney Productions. *Davy Crockett, King of the Wild Frontier*. Feature film made from first three television shows. With Fess Parker and Buddy Ebsen starring, Bill Walsh producer, 1955. Shortened and re-released, 1978.

Republic Pictures. *The Last Command*. With Arthur Hunnicut as Crockett, 1955.

United Artists. *The Alamo*. With John Wayne, Laurence Harvy, and Richard Widmark. Directed by John Wayne, 1960.

CBS Television. *Thirteen Days To Glory*. Directed by Burt Kennedy, with Brian Keith as Crockett, 1987.

INDEX

69